This
Big Book
Christmas
Coloring Pages

BELONGS TO

For the best results use coloring pencils to prevent bleed-through on each page.
If using markers then place a blank sheet of paper behind the page you are coloring to prevent the color from running into the next image.

Copyright © 2020 by Darby Yates

ISBN: 9798691772627

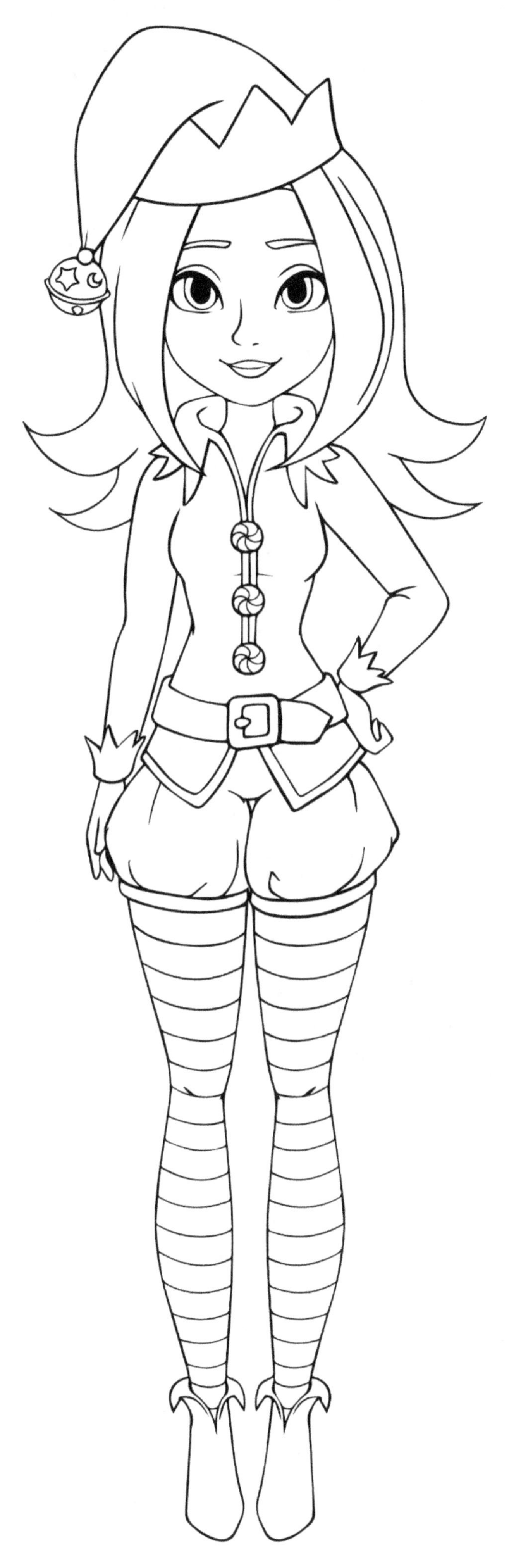

HOLIDAY GIFTS
FAVOURITE SWEATERS
SNOW GLOBES
SKATING
TANGERINES
PINE TREES
COLORFUL SWEETS
NEW YEAR PARTIES
COLORFUL GARLANDS
MILK & GINGER COOKIES
GREETING POSTCARDS
MARSHMALLOW COCOA
PINE CONES
SNOWFLAKES
MULLED WINE
yule log
SEASONAL MUSIC
CHRISTMAS STOCKINGS

wine
MERRY CHRISTMAS

the most
MAGIC
TIME
of the year

WARM WISHES

and

holiday

HUGS